עקב

Ekev

Weekday and Shabbat Afternoon Edition

Elliott Michaelson

MAJS

Copyright Information

I0190614

TRANSLITERATIONS OF HEBREW VOWEL SOUNDS

(A very handy reference guide...)

E

Same sound as:
SPECIAL
THEM
HEAD

* Note that the *Shva* can also indicate the absence of a vowel sound.

O

Same sound as:
HOPE
GROW
BOAT

A

Same sound as:
CUP
TROUBLE
SUPPER

U

Same sound as:
NOODLES
GROUP
SUPER

I

Same sound as:
MEATBALL
PIECE
AGREE

AY

Same sound as:
THEY
AGENT
STEAK

* Some pronounce the *Tzayreh* as "E", some pronounce it as "AY", and some use both pronunciations.

AI

Same sound as:
EYEBALL
RIGHT
LIBRARY

Our *Bar/Bat Mitzvah Survival Guides* use the proper Hebrew names for people and places. The transliterations on this page will help you pronounce them properly. Sometimes, the English and Hebrew names are very close, but often they're quite different. Here are some of the most common differences.

Ashur	Assyria
Bavel	Babylon
Mitzra'im	Egypt
Moshe	Moses
Rivkah	Rebekah
Sha'ul	Saul
Shlomo	Solomon
Ya'akov	Jacob
Yehezk'el	Ezekiel
Yehoshu'a	Joshua
Yehudah	Judah
Yerushalayim	Jerusalem
Yirmiyahu	Jeremiah
Yish'ayah	Isaiah
Yisra'el	Israel
Yitzhak	Isaac
Yosef	Joseph

WHAT'S IN THIS BOOK?

Vital Statistics	
Full text reference:	*Devarim / Deuteronomy 7: 12 to 11: 25*
First Aliyah:	*Devarim / Deuteronomy 7: 12-21*
Second Aliyah:	*Devarim / Deuteronomy 7: 22 to 8: 3*
Third Aliyah:	*Devarim / Deuteronomy 8: 3-10*

Note: the English retelling of the Torah is for the entire parashah, not just the Shabbat pm / Weekday readings. The English for these readings consists of the first part of the retelling.

MY PROGRESS

Date	Torah blessings	Torah reading	Torah review in English

Date	Torah blessings	Torah reading	Torah review in English

Date	Torah blessings	Torah reading	Torah review in English

Date	Torah blessings	Torah reading	Torah review in English

BEFORE YOU BEGIN: GOOD THINGS TO ASK ABOUT THIS BOOK

Welcome to your Bar/Bat Mitzvah Survival Guide! There are some unique features about this guide that might be useful to you during your studies, such as...

What's up with the names of people and places?

Brace yourself, for what I'm about to say (or write, actually) may come as a shock. THE TORAH IS WRITTEN IN HEBREW. Big surprise, I know. So here's the issue many of my students have: in English, we call him *Moses* but in the Torah, we call him *Moshe*. The first woman on Earth is called *Eve* but in Hebrew, she's called *Hava*. The Jews were slaves in *Egypt* — or was it *Mitzra'im*? The answer is both. To try to avoid this confusion between English and Hebrew names, I've decided to stick with the Hebrew. So מֹשֶׁה is translated as *Moshe*, not *Moses*, and יְרוּשָׁלַיִם is *Yerushalayim*, not *Jerusalem*. For more on how to pronounce the Hebrew names, check out the handy translation chart on page ten.

How do you show God talking?

Many of us think of God as an inspirational force in our lives, but how many of us have actual physical conversations with God? As a kid, I was always confused by the fact that God physically speaks to people in the Torah but not to us today. When the Torah records God's "speech", we don't have to think of it as physical words all the time. Moses Maimonides was one of the greatest philosophers and teachers in Judaism, and 800 years ago he famously taught that all divine language in the Torah is metaphorical. Taking that to heart, I've done my very best to express that in my English retellings. God's "dialogue" is written in a different font and with a different tone, and I avoid using direct language like "said" or "told". So did Avraham hear the actual voice of God, or did God act as Avraham's inspirational inner voice? Both beliefs are valid, and it's something I encourage you to explore with your family and your teacher / rabbi.

In these retellings, I refer to God by two proper nouns: *Adonai* and *Elohim*. *Adonai* is God's actual, personal name: י-ה-ו-ה. You'll find it all over the place in the Tanah and in many sidurim. *Elohim* (אֱלֹהִים) is the Hebrew word for "God". Since the Tanah uses both as personal names for God, I've decided to keep the proper Hebrew terms.

What about commentary and translation?

Judaism has always accepted that the Torah text contains four layers of understanding. There's the literal, basic text that you see in front of you (peshat), but underneath the basic text are three layers of metaphorical understanding just waiting to be discovered (derash, remez, sod). You have over two thousand years of scholarship and commentary — including some great stuff being written today — to help you discover these hidden meanings. I've deliberately avoided providing them here for one all-important reason: any commentaries I select would reflect *my* perspective on the text and how it should be taught, and I want you to be free to find *your own way*. That's why I'm leaving the selection of commentary up to you and your rabbi / teacher.

Instead, I've devoted my time to a careful retelling of the Torah and Haftarah texts in English. This isn't a strict translation, but it isn't a sanitized children's version, either. My aim is to provide an English format that flows as easily as a work of juvenile literature, but which preserves the content and significance of the Biblical text. I've also included suggestions for study and analysis that are based on media literacy expectations from public school programs. These blurbs usually address social and historical questions that my own students ask because they need help understanding the ancient society that produced our sacred texts. None of this replaces Rabbinic commentary, but first you need to understand a little bit about the world of our ancient cousins. Then you can work with your rabbi / teacher to find the commentaries that speak to your own interests and concerns.

Da Links!

If you're using the ebook version of this book, try tapping the hyperlinks that appear periodically in the text. Some of them will take you to useful Google maps of many of the locations mentioned in the Torah, while others will take you the *Jewish Virtual Library* or *My Jewish Learning* to learn more about the famous people and nations from the Torah and Haftarah. Enjoy!

-- EM, fall 2015

PUTTING ON THE TALLIT & TEFILLIN

If you've never had the chance to put on the *tallit* or *tefillin*, this is your lucky day! Traditionally, the *tallit* and *tefillin* are worn for all weekday morning services. On Shabbat and Holy Day mornings, only the *tallit* is worn (except Yom Kippur, when we wear the tallit all day). Why the difference? There are many explanations. My favorite reason goes like this: the Torah teaches us to wear reminders of our Divine Agreement with God on our arms and our heads (i.e. *tefillin*). On Shabbat, Pesah, Shavu'ot, Sukkot, Rosh Hashanah, and Yom Kippur, we perform rituals all day long that remind us of God's Agreement with us, so we don't need the *tefillin* to remind us. To put everything on, follow these basic steps. You can also find a video on our website at **http://www.adventurejudaism.net/Bar_Bat_Mitzvah_Guides.html**.

Recite the brahah for wrapping yourself in the tallit.

1

בָּרוּךְ אַתָּה יְיָ אֱלֹהֵינוּ מֶלֶךְ הָעוֹלָם, אֲשֶׁר קִדְּשָׁנוּ בְּמִצְוֹתָיו, וְצִוָּנוּ לְהִתְעַטֵּף בַּצִּיצִת.

We praise You, Adonai our God, Ruler of the universe, whose *mitzvot* make us holy, and who commanded us to cover ourselves with *tzitzit*.

Wrap the collar around your shoulders as if you were putting on a cape.

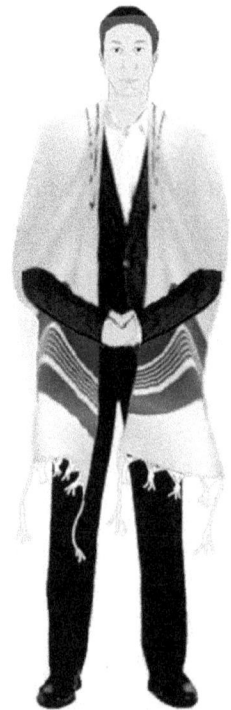

2

On Shabbat and Holy Day mornings, stop here!

3

Loop the *tefillin shel yad* (the one with the extra-long strap) around your bicep.

If you're left-handed, use your right bicep. If you're right-handed, use your left bicep. If you're ambidextrous like me, take your pick!

4

Before tightening the loop, recite this brahah.

בָּרוּךְ אַתָּה יְיָ אֱלֹהֵינוּ מֶלֶךְ הָעוֹלָם, אֲשֶׁר קִדְּשָׁנוּ בְּמִצְוֹתָיו, וְצִוָּנוּ לְהָנִיחַ תְּפִלִּין.

We praise You, Adonai our God, Ruler of the universe, whose *mitzvot* make us holy, and who commanded us to put on *tefillin*.

5

Tighten the loop around your bicep and wrap the strap around your forearm 7 times.

If the strap is long enough, use the extra length to keep the *tefillin* box in place on your bicep.

Wrap the strap around your forearm 7 times.

6

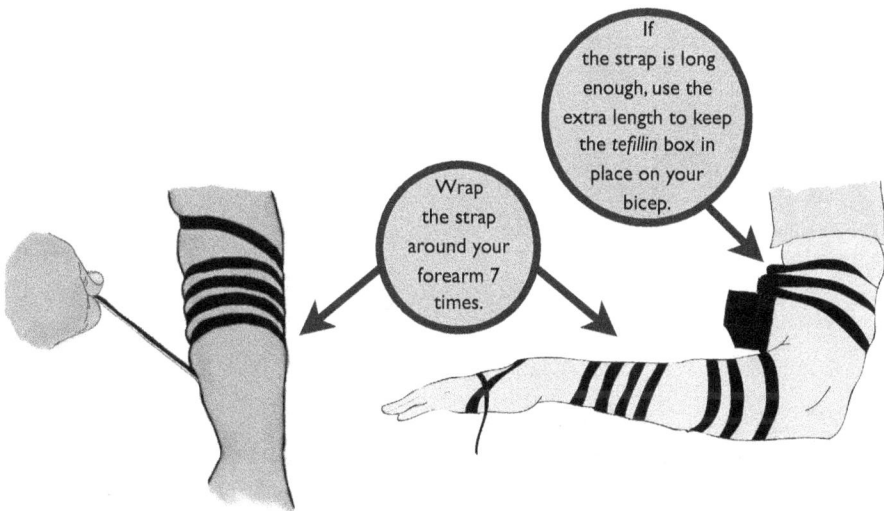

Place the *tefillin shel rosh* at the center of your forehead, right at the hairline.

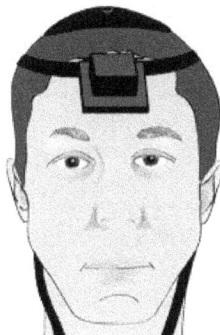

Two long straps extend from the back of the *tefillin shel rosh*. Let them hang freely on either side of your head.

7

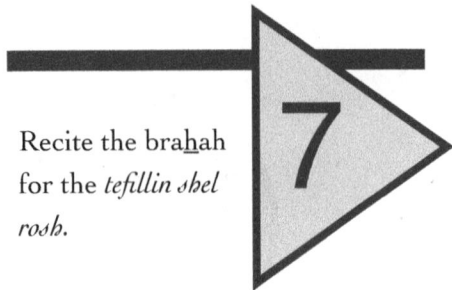

Recite the bra<u>h</u>ah for the *tefillin shel rosh*.

בָּרוּךְ אַתָּה יְיָ אֱלֹהֵינוּ מֶלֶךְ הָעוֹלָם, אֲשֶׁר קִדְּשָׁנוּ בְּמִצְוֹתָיו, וְצִוָּנוּ עַל מִצְוַת תְּפִלִּין.

We praise You, Adonai our God, Ruler of the universe, whose *mitzvot* make us holy, and who commanded the *mitzvah* of tefillin.

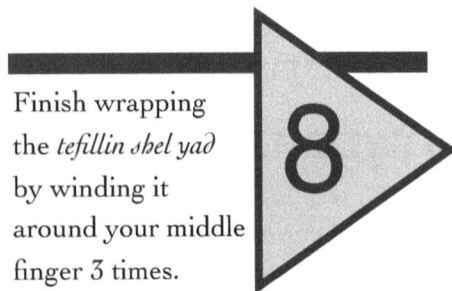

8

Finish wrapping the *tefillin shel yad* by winding it around your middle finger 3 times.

If the strap is long enough, you can also wind it around your hand to help keep everything in place.

Tefillin shel rosh with the two hanging straps.

Tefillin shel yad around the bicep (under the tallit.)

Tefillin shel yad wrapped 3 times around the middle finger.

Tefillin shel yad wrapped 7 times around the forearm.

You're ready to go! When you're finished, take everything off in the reverse order.

TORAH IN ENGLISH: DEVARIM / DEUTERONOMY 7: 12 TO 11: 25

The Wondering Jew Asks...

What's the story so far?

It's been four generations since the final events of the book of *Bereshit / Genesis*. The family that began with Avraham & Sarah, Yitzhak & Rivkah, and the twelve sons of Ya'akov, Le'ah & Rahel, has now grown into the twelve tribes of Benay Yisra'el. A nation that has known great suffering, they have been rescued from slavery in Mitzra'im (Egypt) by Adonai and Adonai's appointed emissary, Moshe. Benay Yisra'el have now been living in the wilderness of Sinai for forty years. Having received God's Laws and Mitzvot (commandments) at Har Sinai (Mount Sinai), and having lived in the wilderness for an entire generation, they prepare to enter the land of Yisra'el.

Meanwhile, Moshe is about to die at the ripe old age of 120. Before he goes, he delivers a series of speeches to remind the people of their Brit (divine agreement) with God. The book of *Devarim* is essentially a record of Moshe's long farewell to his people.

What can I expect from this parashah?

This parashah continues Moshe's second speech to Benay Yisra'el that began in the last parashah, *Va-Ethanan*. Moshe focuses on the benefits of keeping the Brit with God, and he warns the people about the dangers of breaking the Brit. The second paragraph of the *Shema* prayer is taken from the end of parashat *Ekev*.

Without further ado, on to the Torah!

Warning: Read this first!

The book of *Devarim* records a series of farewell speeches that Moshe presents to Benay Yisra'el before he dies. Even though the book is broken into weekly parashot, there are no natural breaks between stories like we see in the books of *Bereshit / Genesis* or *Bamidbar / Numbers*. Instead, *Devarim* flows from one theme to the next. Parashat *Ekev's* themes are in **bold:** recalling what God did for us in the past → reviewing the Brit and our divine connection with God → **benefits of keeping the Brit** → **warnings about breaking the Brit** → religious obligations in the Brit → rules for leaders → rules for creating a just society → punishments for breaking the Brit → rewards for keeping the Brit → pleading with Benay Yisra'el to keep the Brit → appointing a successor → recording Moshe's words for posterity → Moshe's final, epic poem → blessing the tribes of Yisra'el → Moshe's death.

To understand what's going on in *Ekev*, you need to know how it connects into the themes before and after.

VERY IMPORTANT NOTE!

THE BIT YOU'RE ABOUT TO READ IS THE END OF THE PREVIOUS PARASHAH, VA-ETHANAN. I'M PRINTING IT HERE BECAUSE THE END OF VA-ETHANAN AND THE BEGINNING OF EKEV ARE ONE SPEECH. IN OTHER WORDS, IT'S HARD TO UNDERSTAND EKEV'S BEGINNING WITHOUT READING VA-ETHANAN'S ENDING. I'LL LET YOU KNOW WHEN EKEV OFFICIALLY STARTS.

CONQUERED PEOPLES

7: 1-5

MOSHE NOW DESCRIBES WHAT TO DO WITH THE PEOPLE BENAY YISRA'EL ARE ABOUT TO DEFEAT...

"After Adonai your God brings you into the land you are about to take charge of...
　"After seven nations larger and more powerful than you are driven out before you
　　(Hitites, Girgashites, Emorites, Cana'anites, Perizites, Hivites, and Yevusites)...
　　　"After Adonai your God hands them to you and you defeat them...

"You will annihilate them! Make no treaties with them and show them no mercy. Do not marry them! Do not give your daughters to their sons or take their daughters for your sons. They will tempt your children to turn away and serve other gods. Then Adonai's rage will fall on you and God will quickly destroy you.

7: 6-8

You will annihilate them: To many modern readers, it looks like God is commanding a genocide, which is exactly what people like Adolf Hitler tried to do to us. It hardly seems fair or ethical. In Ye Olden Dayes, this kind of total destruction was occasionally used by kingdoms to demonstrate their power and to warn other nations to do what they're told. From this perspective, the command to destroy our enemies is consistent with the way warfare was sometimes done. That said, the Biblical books that tell the history of the Israelite kingdoms after Moshe's time clearly show that this total annihilation never actually happened. Your rabbi / teacher can help you explore these ideas.

"You are a holy people to Adonai your God because Adonai chose you from all the nations on earth to be God's treasured people. Adonai didn't favor you with love or choose you because you were more numerous than the others. In fact, you were the smallest! It was out of love and because of the promise to your ancestors that Adonai rescued you with a mighty hand from the house of slavery, from the rule of Par'oh king of Mitzra'im.

7: 9-11

"Therefore, always know that Adonai your God is the faithful God Who keeps the Brit. God's divine compassion stretches to the thousandth generation for those who love God and obey God's Mitzvot, but God repays with immediate destruction those who hate God. So follow the Mitzvot, the Laws, and the Rules just as I've commanded you today."

"Obey them!"

AND NOW, ON TO PARASHAT EKEV...

MEMBER BENEFITS

If you listen to these Rules, if you keep them and obey them, then Adonai your God will keep the **Brit** and the kindness that was promised to your ancestors. God will be loyal to you, bless you, and make you numerous. Your children, crops, and grain and oil harvests will be blessed. Your flocks and herds will multiply on the land that God swore to your ancestors would be given to you.

Brit: The בְּרִית is the Agreement between Adonai and the people of Yisra'el. Adonai promised to provide wealth, land, healthy harvests, and security, and in exchange Yisra'el agreed to follow the Mitzvot. For an example of the Brit that Moshe is talking about here, check out chapter 19 of *Shemot / Exodus*. Brit is usually translated as "Covenant".

Barren: This means that someone is unable to have children. In Ye Olden Dayes, having many children symbolized prosperity and security.

Mitzra'im: a.k.a. Egypt.

You will be more blessed than any other nation. No man, woman, or animal will be **barren**. Adonai will take away all sickness; the diseases that plagued **Mitzra'im** will never affect you. They will only affect your enemies.

You will consume all the nations that Adonai your God delivers to you. Show them no pity! Their gods will lure you away, so don't serve them!

You might ask yourself, "These nations are bigger than me, how can I drive them out?" Don't fear them! Remember well what Adonai your God did to **Par'oh** and all of Mitzra'im: **the great tests, signs, and wonders you witnessed with your own eyes, and the way Adonai your God brought you out with an outstretched arm.** This is what Adonai will do to any nation you fear!

Then Adonai will send swarms of

Par'oh: a.k.a. Pharaoh.

The great tests, signs...: Moshe is reminding Benay Yisra'el of a series of very famous events that happened to them a generation earlier. Ever since, these events have been (and continue to be) commemorated every spring in an equally famous week-long festival. Which event and festival are we talking about? See if you can figure it out. Hint: check out the first half of the book of *Shemot / Exodus* for details.

Outstretched arm: This is a poetic way of describing strength and power. If God isn't a person, why does Moshe describe God as having arms? The Tanah often uses images of the human body to make statements about God. Why do you think this is? How did this help our ancient cousins express their ideas? Your rabbi / teacher can help you explore this.

wasps against any survivors and anyone who was hiding. They will be destroyed before you. Adonai who is great and terrifying is with you, so don't fear your enemies.

Adonai your God will drive out those nations gradually because if you defeat them too quickly, then wild animals will multiply everywhere. Rest assured that Adonai will deliver all of your enemies to you with great destruction until they're **wiped out**. God will hand their chieftains over to you, and their names will be erased from history. No-one will stand in your way as you completely destroy them.

> **Wiped out:** The idea of totally wiping out our enemies can make some modern readers feel very uncomfortable. Jewish tradition promotes the idea of reading the Torah as midrash (metaphor), so that our "enemies" might represent our worst impulses. From this point of view, what might Moshe mean when he commands Yisra'el to wipe them out? Your rabbi / teacher can help you explore this idea.

Burn their idols to ash! Don't be lured away by the silver and gold that decorate these idols, for they are an outrage to Adonai your God! If you bring an outrage into your home, you will be cursed with destruction along with it! You will treat it with utter disgust, for it is marked for destruction.

REMEMBER WHAT GOD DID FOR YOU

Take care to observe all of the Mitzvot I'm commanding you today. Do this so that you'll inherit the land that Adonai promised to your ancestors and prosper in it. Remember the path Adonai led you on these forty years in the wilderness: a path of great difficulty to see what was in your hearts, a path to test you to see whether or not you would keep God's Mitzvot.

> **Mana:** This was a seedy food that God provided to Benay Yisra'el. It appeared miraculously on the ground every morning, and they would collect enough to feed themselves for the day (on the day before Shabbat, they'd collect a double portion, since no mana fell on Shabbat). For details, see chapter 16 of the book of *Shemot / Exodus*.
>
> **Survive on bread... Adonai chooses:** Bread isn't a natural food. There's no such thing as a plant that grows bread. Bread is made by combining ingredients that grow naturally, shaping them, and baking them. Moshe's point here seems to be that our survival doesn't depend on what we make with our own hands; rather, we can survive on anything that God tells us to eat.

God tested you with the hardship of hunger by feeding you **mana**, a food which neither you nor your ancestors knew about. This was done to teach you that humankind does not **survive on bread alone, but on whatever Adonai chooses**.

During those forty years, your clothes didn't wear out and your feet never blistered! Keep in mind that Adonai your God sets consequences for you just as a parent sets consequences for a child. You will keep Adonai's Mitzvot, walk in God's path, and be in awe of God.

Adonai your God is bringing you to a fertile
land:

> A land with streams, springs, and
> fountains flowing from valleys and hills;
>
> A land with wheat, barley, grape vines, fig
> trees, and pomegranates;
>
> A land of olive groves and honey;
>
> A land where you will lack nothing and never
> be short on food;
>
> A land where the very stones are iron and
> you'll mine copper in the hills.

**You will eat and be satisfied, and you will
bless Adonai your God for the fertile land God
has given you.**

You will eat and be satisfied...: In Hebrew, verse 10
looks like this:

וְאָכַלְתָּ וְשָׂבָעְתָּ וּבֵרַכְתָּ אֶת-יי אֱלֹהֶיךָ
עַל-הָאָרֶץ הַטֹּבָה אֲשֶׁר נָתַן-לָךְ

This is used in the second blessing of the traditional *Birkat
Ha-mazon*, which is a series of blessings that many Jews
recite after every meal. After reciting this line, the blessing
praises God for our land and for our food. By writing the
Birkat Ha-mazon in this way, the early rabbis made sure that
Moshe's command would be followed.

Explore other examples where our liturgy is used to fulfill
commands from the Torah. Ask your rabbi / teacher for help.

DON'T FORGET ABOUT GOD. OR ELSE...

8: 11-16

Be careful not to forget Adonai your God by ignoring the Mitzvot, Rules, and Laws that I'm
commanding you right now!

> When you have eaten and are satisfied,
>
> > When your herds and flocks have grown in size,
> >
> > > When your silver and gold and everything you own have increased,
>
> Then you may become arrogant and forget Adonai your God —
>
> > Who brought you out of Mitzra'im, a land of slavery,
> >
> > > Who guided you through a huge, terrible wilderness filled with poisonous snakes, scorpions, and
> > > parched ground,
> > >
> > > > Who made water come out of flint rock for you,
> > > >
> > > > > Who fed you mana — a food unknown to you or your ancestors, to test you so you might
> > > > > benefit from it in the future.

You might say to yourself, "I got this wealth from my own power and from the strength of my own hand!" You must remember that it was Adonai your God Who gave you the power to amass your wealth, in order to fulfill the Brit that God promised to your ancestors, just as it is today.

In the future, if you truly forget Adonai your God, if you follow the paths of other gods by serving them and worshipping them, I warn you now that you will surely be destroyed. If you fail to listen to the Voice of Adonai your God, you'll be wiped out just like the nations Adonai is wiping out for you.

ERUPTIONS OF ANGER

9: 1-5

Hear this, Yisra'el: today you will cross over the Yarden River to push out nations that are bigger and more powerful than you, with towns that are fortified up to the sky, with people who descend from the mythical **Anakites** just like in the old saying, "Who can withstand the children of Anak?"

> **Anakites:** The עֲנָקִים were mythological giants. Our ancient cousins could have been describing a group of unusually large people or they may have meant actual giants. Some interpretations see this as a way of making the people of Cana'an seem really intimidating.
>
> **The Promise:** a.k.a the Brit (Covenant) with God. For details on these Promise, see chapters 17, 26, and 35 of the book of *Bereshit / Genesis*.

Know that Adonai your God will cross over ahead of you. Like a consuming fire, God will destroy them and topple them for you so you can push them out and eradicate them quickly, just as Adonai told you to.

After Adonai your God has cleared them away for you, don't say to yourself, "Adonai has brought me to inherit this land because of my righteousness" or "Adonai drove out the other nations because of their wicked behavior". You aren't inheriting this land because of your righteousness or because of your proper behavior! Adonai your God drove them out because of their wickedness and because of **the Promise** God swore to your ancestors Avraham, Yitzhak, and Ya'akov!

So Adonai your God isn't giving you this great land because of your righteousness. You're stubborn and prideful! Remember — don't forget! — how you made Adonai furious from the moment you left Mitzra'im until you came here. You rebelled against God all the time you were in the wilderness! At **Horev** you made Adonai so angry that God was ready to destroy you. When I was up on the mountain to receive the stone tablets of the Brit, I stayed there for forty days and nights with no food or water. The tablets that Adonai gave to me were a record of Adonai's Message to you. They came from the fires of the mountaintop on the day you all gathered together, written by the Finger of God!

> **Horev:** a.k.a Mount Sinai.
>
> For details on what happened at Horev, check out chapters 31-34 of the book of *Shemot / Exodus*.

At the end of the forty days and nights, Adonai presented the two tablets of the Brit to me along with this Message:

Get up and hurry down from here! The people you brought out of Mitzra'im have become corrupt. They have run away from My Path and made an idol for themselves!

Then Adonai added:

I see that this nation is stubborn and prideful! Leave Me alone so I can eradicate them and erase their name from under the heavens! I will make a nation from you that will be greater and mightier than them!

So I turned away and climbed down the mountain as it brimmed with fire, the two stone tablets of the Brit in my arms. Then I saw the terrible crime you'd committed against Adonai your God: you'd made a calf out of molten metal. You really had run away from what Adonai commanded you to do! Then I held up the stone tablets and hurled them to the ground. You watched me smash them.

I bent low to the ground before Adonai, just as I did at the beginning of my forty days and nights. I refused food and water because of your crime — because you provoked Adonai's rage by doing what God considered to be an evil thing. I was afraid of the vengeful anger that Adonai felt towards you, the anger that would cause your destruction. But Adonai listened to me at that time, too! Adonai was also furious with Aharon and wanted to kill him, so I prayed for Aharon's life, as well.

I threw the calf you made into the fire, broke it to pieces, and ground it to a powder. Then I dumped it into the stream that flowed down from the mountain.

9: 22-24

You also provoked Adonai at **Tav'erah, Masah, and Kivrot-Hata'avah!** Later, when Adonai sent you up from **Kadesh-Barne'a** with this order:

Take control of the land which I am

giving to you!

You ignored it, you lost faith, and you didn't listen to God's Voice. You've been disobedient for as long as I've known you!

Tav'erah...: These are names that were given to places where Benay Yisra'el rebelled against God after they left Mount Sinai. They mean "Burning", "Temptation", and "Graves of Craving". For details on the burning temptations and cravings, check out chapter 11 of the book of *Bamidbar / Numbers*.

Kadesh-Barne'a: This was a town in the far south of ancient Israel near modern-day Eilat. Moshe is referring to the time when he sent twelve spies into the land to scout the people living there, and ten of the spies came back with such a negative report that Benay Yisra'el lost faith in God. For details, see chapters 13 and 14 of *Bamidbar / Numbers*.

9: 25-29

For forty days and nights I bowed low before Adonai because Adonai threatened to wipe you out! I prayed to Adonai: "My Lord, Adonai, don't destroy Your people," I begged. "Don't destroy the Legacy that You, in Your greatness, rescued — that You brought out of Mitzra'im with a mighty hand! Remember Your servants Avraham, Yitzhak, and Ya'akov. Overlook this nation's stubbornness, its wickedness, and its crimes. Otherwise, the people of the land you rescued us from will say, 'They were brought to the wilderness to die because Adonai was unable to bring them the Promised Land, because Adonai hated them!' But they are Your People and Your Legacy. You saved them with great power and an outstretched arm."

Then Adonai replied:

Carve two stone tablets just like the first ones and return to Me on the mountain. Build an Aron out of wood. I will rewrite the words that were on the first set of tablets that you broke and you will place them in the Aron.

Aron: The אָרוֹן was the large, extremely fancy chest that held the written records of God's Mitzvot from Mount Sinai. It was coated with gold, and two golden Keruvim decorated the top. A Keruv was a mythical winged creature with human and animal features. The Tanah isn't entirely clear as to exactly what Keruvim looked like, but our ancestors certainly knew. The Keruvim faced each other from opposite ends of the Aron and had their wings stretched out with the tips touching. God's Messages came to Moshe from between these two Keruvim. What do synagogues use today in place of this Aron? Explore the differences and similarities.

So I made the Aron out of wood, carved two new stone tablets, and headed back up the mountain with the tablets in my arms. Adonai recorded again the ten instructions that God spoke to you out of the fire on the day of the communal assembly, and then gave them to me. I came back down and put the tablets in the Aron, which is where they are right now according to Adonai's command.

Benay Yisra'el traveled from Be'erot Benay-Ya'akan to Moserah, where Aharon died. He was buried there, and we made his son, El'azar, the Kohen Ha-Gadol in his place. From there they went to Gudgod, and then on to Yotvatah, which was an area with streams of running water. That was when Adonai separated the tribe of Levi from the rest of the community, giving them the responsibilities of carrying the Aron, serving Adonai's needs, and blessing God's Name, just as they continue to do

Moshe does a strange thing here. He switches from talking about the tribes of Yisra'el in the plural to talking about them as if they were individuals. This isn't a typo. In Ye Olden Dayes, tribes and nations often traced their origins to individual people. So when Moshe says that "Levi has no inheritance like his brothers have", he isn't talking about the actual Levi and Levi's actual brothers. Moshe is talking about the tribes as a whole.

This is why Levi has no inheritance...: The tribe of Levi was in charge of all the religious and ritual leadership. Because of this, they weren't granted territory in the land of Yisra'el. Instead, they lived in special villages throughout all the tribal territories.

today. **This is why Levi has no inheritance like his brothers have.** Adonai is his inheritance, just as Adonai your God instructed him.

Anyway, I stayed on the mountain for forty days and nights like I did the first time. Adonai listened to me just like before, and didn't destroy you. Adonai's Message to me was:

Get up and lead the people to take control of the land I promised their ancestors I would give them.

LOYALTY PROGRAM

10: 12-16

So, Yisra'el, what does Adonai your God demand? That you should treat God with great reverence, that you should walk God's Path, that you should be completely loyal and serve Adonai your God with your whole heart and every fibre of your being. Observe Adonai's Mitzvot and Laws that I'm commanding you today so that everything will go well for you.

So cut away...: The Hebrew in verse 16 actually says, "circumcise the foreskin of your hearts". In a very poetic way, Moshe is telling us that the Brit we have with God must be physical and spiritual.

Don't the heavens, the heavens above the heavens, and all the world and all that's in it belong to Adonai? Yet Adonai made this bond of unswerving loyalty only with your ancestors! God chose their descendants over all the other nations, and God continues to do this today! **So cut away whatever makes you stiffen your hearts** and stop being so cruel and difficult!

10: 17-22

Your God, Adonai, is the God of all gods and the Master of all masters: the great, mighty, awe-inspiring God Who shows no favor and cannot be bribed. God brings justice to orphans, widows, and those who lovingly care for outsiders by providing food and clothing. Take special care of outsiders, for you were once outsiders in the land of Mitzra'im!

As numerous as the stars in the heavens: This hardly looks impressive to those of us who live in an urban area today. But in ancient times there was no light pollution. A person looking to the sky would see thousands of stars — far too many to count. To experience this today, you need to visit a dark sky sanctuary or a place that's at least an hour away from city lights. Or you could camp out in the Negev or the Sinai like our ancestors did!

Show great reverence for Adonai your God. Worship God, stick with God, and swear only by God's Name. Adonai is your praise, your god, the One who did the amazing and wondrous things you saw with your own eyes! When your ancestors went down to Mitzra'im, they were only seventy people; now Adonai your God has made you **as numerous as the stars in the heavens.**

So you must show your unswerving loyalty for Adonai your God by always supporting God's Priorities, Laws, Rules, and Mitzvot. Understand that I'm not talking to your descendants who don't relate to this, who haven't experienced

> **Datan, Aviram, the clan of Eliyav:** Moshe is referring to the famous rebellion led by Moshe's first cousin, Korah. Datan, Aviram, and the clan of Eliyav were Korah's co-conspirators. For details, see chapter sixteen of the book of *Bamidbar / Numbers*.

Adonai's consequences and greatness, or God's mighty hand and outstretched arm, or the wonders and signs that God did in Mitzra'im to Par'oh and his country, or what God did to Mitzra'im's army and cavalry and chariots by drowning them in the waters of the Reed Sea, or what God did to you in the wilderness before you came here, or what God did to **Datan, Aviram, the clan of Eliyav** from the tribe of Re'uven — how the ground opened its mouth and swallowed them, their households and homes, and every living thing they had, right in the midst of all of Yisra'el! Only YOUR eyes have seen all the incredible things that Adonai did!

So you must observe the Mitzvah I'm commanding to you right now so that you'll be powerful enough to hold the territory you're about to cross the river to take control of. Do this, and you'll lengthen the time you have to live in this land that Adonai promised to your ancestors and their descendants — **a land flowing with milk and honey.**

The land you're about to take over isn't like the land you just came from. In

> **A land flowing with milk and honey:** This is a very famous line Moshe and God use to poetically describe the land of Yisra'el as a kind of paradise.
>
> **The seeds you planted...soaks up heaven's rain:** Moshe is comparing farming in Egypt and Israel. Egypt's agriculture is based on annual flooding of the Nile River. Egyptians dig channels from the Nile to their fields to irrigate their crops. Israel has rugged hills divided by deep ravines. Water for farming is soaked up by the earth and comes out in springs and wells. How does this help you understand what Moshe is saying here?

Mitzra'im, **the seeds you planted had to be watered manually like a vegetable garden, but the place you're going to is a land of hills and ravines that soaks up heaven's rain.** It's a land that Adonai your God constantly keeps watch over from the beginning of the year to the end.

In the future, if you listen carefully to the Mitzvot I'm commanding you today, to be completely loyal to Adonai by serving your God with your whole heart and every fibre of your being:

> I will cause the late fall and early
> spring rains to come on time so that
> you may harvest your grain, your wine,
> and your oil. I will cause grass to grow
> in your fields for your animals so you
> may eat and have enough.

Verses 13 to 21 form the second paragraph of the original version of the *Shema* prayer. The full *Shema* includes *Devarim* 6: 4-9, *Devarim* 11: 13-21, and *Bamidbar* 15: 37-41. These three sections form a guide that's designed to provide a basic blueprint for maintaining Jewish continuity. Why did the ancient rabbis choose these three sections? How do these sections work together to accomplish this goal? Ask your rabbi / teacher about this.

The original form of the *Shema* was developed over 2000 years ago. If you had to develop a basic guide for Jewish continuity for today, which three sections of Torah would you include? Explore your ideas!

Watch yourselves carefully so that your hearts don't turn away to serve other gods and worship them! If you do, Adonai's anger will flare against you. The heavens will close up so there's no rain, the earth won't grow crops, and you will quickly disappear from this bountiful land that Adonai has given to you.

Keep my lessons in your heart and soul. Keep them as symbols for your arms and as **totafot** between your eyes. Teach them to your children. Keep them in mind when you're resting at home, when you're out during the day, when you go to sleep at night and when you wake up in the morning. Carve them into the **doorposts** of your homes and your gates. Do this so that the time that you and your descendants live here will be lengthened

Totafot: No-one's completely sure what טֹטָפֹת originally were. The word only appears three times in the Tana<u>h</u> (Jewish Bible), and each time it refers to an object we wrap around our heads and which rests between our eyes. Hence, the tefillin shel rosh (tefillin for our head). There are four Torah texts inside each tefillin box, including this one right here. See if you can find the other three (your rabbi / teacher can help).

Doorposts: The Hebrew word for this is מְזֻזֹת. Hanging a mezuzah on our front doors is still a widespread Jewish custom. Which Torah texts are inside the mezuzah? Take a wild guess... ☺

— the land that Adonai swore to your ancestors would be given to you as long as there is a heaven above the earth.

11:22-25
This is the
Maftir reading.

If you are very dedicated to keeping these orders I'm commanding you today, if you do them and love Adonai your God, walk God's Path and stay with God, then Adonai will drive away the nations who defy you, nations that are greater and mightier than you. Every place your feet touch will be yours. Your borders will stretch from the wilderness to the **Levanon**, from the **River Perat** to the **Great Sea**. No-one will oppose you, for Adonai your God will spread the fear of you across the land you walk on, just as God told you.

Levanon: This was (and still is) a heavily forested region just north of modern-day Israel in the modern-day country of... you guessed it... Lebanon!

River Perat: This is the Hebrew name for the Euphrates, which flows through modern-day Iraq and Syria.

Great Sea: a.k.a Mediterranean Sea.

The territory described here includes areas of modern-day Lebanon and Syria. For other descriptions of the Promised Land's borders, see chapter 15 of *Bereshit*, chapter 23 of *Shemot*, chapter 34 of *Bamidbar*, and chapter 19 of *Devarim*. Other Biblical books like *Shemu'el* and *Yehezk'el* also offer varying descriptions of Yisra'el's borders.

Up next...

Re'eh! Moshe's huge farewell speech continues as he describes the religious obligations that are part of the Brit with God.

TORAH AND BLESSINGS IN HEBREW: DEVARIM / DEUTERONOMY 7: 12 TO 8: 10

Before the Torah reading, recite one of the following blessings.
Your rabbi or teacher will tell you which one is appropriate for your community.

You call out:	**You call out:**
בָּרְכוּ אֶת יְיָ הַמְבֹרָךְ.	בָּרְכוּ אֶת יְיָ הַמְבֹרָךְ.
The congregation responds:	**The congregation responds:**
בָּרוּךְ יְיָ הַמְבֹרָךְ לְעוֹלָם וָעֶד.	בָּרוּךְ יְיָ הַמְבֹרָךְ לְעוֹלָם וָעֶד.
You say it back to them:	**You say it back to them:**
בָּרוּךְ יְיָ הַמְבֹרָךְ לְעוֹלָם וָעֶד.	בָּרוּךְ יְיָ הַמְבֹרָךְ לְעוֹלָם וָעֶד.
You continue:	**You continue:**
בָּרוּךְ אַתָּה יְיָ אֱלֹהֵינוּ מֶלֶךְ הָעוֹלָם, אֲשֶׁר קֵרְבָנוּ לַעֲבוֹדָתוֹ וְנָתַן לָנוּ אֶת תּוֹרָתוֹ. בָּרוּךְ אַתָּה יְיָ, נוֹתֵן הַתּוֹרָה.	בָּרוּךְ אַתָּה יְיָ אֱלֹהֵינוּ מֶלֶךְ הָעוֹלָם, אֲשֶׁר בָּחַר בָּנוּ מִכָּל הָעַמִּים וְנָתַן לָנוּ אֶת תּוֹרָתוֹ. בָּרוּךְ אַתָּה יְיָ, נוֹתֵן הַתּוֹרָה.
Let us praise Adonai, the Blessed One!	Let us praise Adonai, the Blessed One!
Let Adonai, the Blessed One, be praised forever!	Let Adonai, the Blessed One, be praised forever!
We praise You, Adonai our God, Ruler of the universe, Who drew us close to God's Work and gave us God's Torah.	We praise You, Adonai our God, Ruler of the universe, Who chose us from all the nations to be given God's Torah.
We praise You, Adonai, the Giver of Torah.	We praise You, Adonai, the Giver of Torah.

18. לֹא תִירָא מֵהֶם

זָכֹר תִּזְכֹּר

אֵת אֲשֶׁר־עָשָׂה יְהוָה אֱלֹהֶיךָ

לְפַרְעֹה וּלְכָל־מִצְרָיִם:

19. הַמַּסֹּת הַגְּדֹלֹת

אֲשֶׁר־רָאוּ עֵינֶיךָ

וְהָאֹתֹת וְהַמֹּפְתִים

וְהַיָּד הַחֲזָקָה וְהַזְּרֹעַ הַנְּטוּיָה

אֲשֶׁר הוֹצִאֲךָ יְהוָה אֱלֹהֶיךָ

כֵּן־יַעֲשֶׂה

יְהוָה אֱלֹהֶיךָ לְכָל־הָעַמִּים

אֲשֶׁר־אַתָּה יָרֵא מִפְּנֵיהֶם:

20. וְגַם אֶת־הַצִּרְעָה

יְשַׁלַּח

יְהוָה אֱלֹהֶיךָ בָּם

עַד־אֲבֹד

הַנִּשְׁאָרִים

וְהַנִּסְתָּרִים מִפָּנֶיךָ:

ישלם לו ושמרת את המצוה ואת
החזקים ואת המשפטים אשר אנכי
מצוך היום לעשותם
והיה עקב תשמעון את המשפטים
האלה ושמרתם ועשיתם אתם ושמר
יהוה אלהיך לך את הברית ואת
החסד אשר נשבע לאבתיך ואהבך
וברכך והרבך וברך פרי בטנך ופרי
אדמתך דגנך ותירשך ויצהרך שגר
אלפיך ועשתרת צאנך על האדמה
אשר נשבע לאבתיך לתת לך ברוך
תהיה מכל העמים לא יהיה בך עקר
ועקרה ובבהמתך והסיר יהוה ממך
כל חלי וכל מדוי מצרים הרעים
אשר ידעת לא ישימם בך ונתנם
בכל שנאיך ואכלת את כל העמים
אשר יהוה אלהיך נתן לך לא תחוס
עינך עליהם ולא תעבד את אלהיהם
כי מוקש הוא לך כי
תאמר בלבבך רבים הגוים האלה
ממני איכה אוכל להורישם לא
תירא מהם זכר תזכר את אשר עשה
יהוה אלהיך לפרעה ולכל
מצרים המסת הגדלת אשר ראו
עיניך והאתת והמפתים והיד החזקה
והזרע הנטויה אשר הוצאך יהוה
אלהיך כן יעשה יהוה אלהיך לכל
העמים אשר אתה ירא מפניהם וגם

Chapter 7

15. וְהֵסִיר יְהוָה
מִמְּךָ כָּל־חֹלִי
וְכָל־מַדְוֵי מִצְרַיִם הָרָעִים
אֲשֶׁר יָדַעְתָּ
לֹא יְשִׂימָם בָּךְ
וּנְתָנָם בְּכָל־שֹׂנְאֶיךָ:

12. וְהָיָה | עֵקֶב תִּשְׁמְעוּן
אֵת הַמִּשְׁפָּטִים הָאֵלֶּה
וּשְׁמַרְתֶּם וַעֲשִׂיתֶם אֹתָם
וְשָׁמַר יְהוָֹה אֱלֹהֶיךָ לְךָ
אֶת־הַבְּרִית וְאֶת־הַחֶסֶד
אֲשֶׁר נִשְׁבַּע לַאֲבֹתֶיךָ:

16. וְאָכַלְתָּ אֶת־כָּל־הָעַמִּים
אֲשֶׁר יְהוָה אֱלֹהֶיךָ נֹתֵן לָךְ
לֹא־תָחוֹס עֵינְךָ עֲלֵיהֶם
וְלֹא תַעֲבֹד אֶת־אֱלֹהֵיהֶם
כִּי־מוֹקֵשׁ הוּא לָךְ:

13. וַאֲהֵבְךָ
וּבֵרַכְךָ וְהִרְבֶּךָ
וּבֵרַךְ פְּרִי־בִטְנְךָ וּפְרִי־אַדְמָתֶךָ
דְּגָנְךָ וְתִירֹשְׁךָ וְיִצְהָרֶךָ
שְׁגַר־אֲלָפֶיךָ וְעַשְׁתְּרֹת צֹאנֶךָ
עַל הָאֲדָמָה
אֲשֶׁר־נִשְׁבַּע לַאֲבֹתֶיךָ לָתֶת לָךְ:

17. כִּי תֹאמַר בִּלְבָבְךָ
רַבִּים
הַגּוֹיִם הָאֵלֶּה מִמֶּנִּי
אֵיכָה אוּכַל לְהוֹרִישָׁם:

14. בָּרוּךְ תִּהְיֶה מִכָּל־הָעַמִּים
לֹא־יִהְיֶה בְךָ
עָקָר וַעֲקָרָה וּבִבְהֶמְתֶּךָ:

2. וְזָכַרְתָּ֣ אֶת־כָּל־הַדֶּ֗רֶךְ
אֲשֶׁ֨ר הוֹלִֽיכְךָ֜
יְהוָ֧ה אֱלֹהֶ֛יךָ
זֶ֜ה
אַרְבָּעִ֥ים שָׁנָ֖ה בַּמִּדְבָּ֑ר
לְמַ֨עַן עַנֹּֽתְךָ֜ לְנַסֹּֽתְךָ֗
לָדַ֜עַת
אֶת־אֲשֶׁ֤ר בִּֽלְבָבְךָ֙
הֲתִשְׁמֹ֥ר מצותו [מִצְוֺתָ֖יו]
אִם־לֹֽא׃

3. וַֽיְעַנְּךָ֮ וַיַּרְעִבֶ֒ךָ֒
וַיַּֽאֲכִֽלְךָ֤ אֶת־הַמָּן֙
אֲשֶׁ֣ר לֹא־יָדַ֔עְתָּ
וְלֹ֥א יָדְע֖וּן אֲבֹתֶ֑יךָ
לְמַ֣עַן הוֹדִֽיעֲךָ֗
כִּ֠י
לֹ֣א עַל־הַלֶּ֤חֶם לְבַדּוֹ֙
יִחְיֶ֣ה הָֽאָדָ֔ם
כִּ֛י
עַל־כָּל־מוֹצָ֥א פִֽי־יְהוָ֖ה
יִחְיֶ֥ה הָאָדָֽם׃

את הצרעה ישלח יהוה אלהיך בם
עד אבד הנשארים והנסתרים
מפניך לא תערץ מפניהם כי יהוה
אלהיך בקרבך אל גדול ונורא ונשל
יהוה אלהיך את הגוים האל מפניך
מעט מעט לא תוכל כלתם מהר פן
תרבה עליך חית השדה ונתנם יהוה
אלהיך לפניך והמם מהומה גדלה
עד השמדם ונתן מלכיהם בידך
והאבדת את שמם מתחת השמים
לא יתיצב איש בפניך עד השמדך
אתם פסילי אלהיהם תשרפון באש
לא תחמד כסף וזהב עליהם ולקחת
לך פן תוקש בו כי תועבת יהוה
אלהיך הוא ולא תביא תועבה אל
ביתך והיית חרם כמהו שקץ תשקצנו
ותעב תתעבנו כי חרם הוא
כל המצוה אשר אנכי מצוך היום
תשמרון לעשות למען תחיון
ורביתם ובאתם וירשתם את הארץ
אשר נשבע יהוה לאבתיכם וזכרת
את כל הדרך אשר הוליכך יהוה
אלהיך זה ארבעים שנה במדבר
למען ענתך לנסתך לדעת את אשר
בלבבך התשמר מצותו אם
לא ויענך וירעבך ויאכלך את המן
אשר לא ידעת ולא ידעון אבתיך
למען הודיעך כי לא על הלחם

כה. פְּסִילֵ֣י אֱלֹהֵיהֶם֮ תִּשְׂרְפ֣וּן בָּאֵ֒שׁ

לֹֽא־תַחְמֹד֩ כֶּ֨סֶף וְזָהָ֤ב עֲלֵיהֶם֙

וְלָקַחְתָּ֣ לָ֔ךְ

פֶּ֚ן תִּוָּקֵ֣שׁ בּ֔וֹ

כִּ֧י תוֹעֲבַ֛ת

יְהֹוָ֥ה אֱלֹהֶ֖יךָ הֽוּא׃

כו. וְלֹא־תָבִ֤יא תֽוֹעֵבָה֙ אֶל־בֵּיתֶ֔ךָ

וְהָיִ֥יתָ חֵ֖רֶם כָּמֹ֑הוּ

שַׁקֵּ֧ץ ׀ תְּשַׁקְּצֶ֛נּוּ

וְתַעֵ֥ב ׀ תְּֽתַעֲבֶ֖נּוּ כִּי־חֵ֥רֶם הֽוּא׃

Chapter 8

א. כׇּל־הַמִּצְוָ֗ה

אֲשֶׁ֨ר אָנֹכִ֧י מְצַוְּךָ֛

הַיּ֖וֹם תִּשְׁמְר֣וּן לַעֲשׂ֑וֹת

לְמַ֨עַן תִּֽחְי֜וּן וּרְבִיתֶ֗ם

וּבָאתֶם֙ וִֽירִשְׁתֶּ֣ם אֶת־הָאָ֔רֶץ

אֲשֶׁר־נִשְׁבַּ֥ע יְהֹוָ֖ה לַאֲבֹתֵיכֶֽם׃

כא. לֹ֥א תַֽעֲרֹ֖ץ מִפְּנֵיהֶ֑ם

כִּֽי־יְהֹוָ֤ה אֱלֹהֶ֙יךָ֙ בְּקִרְבֶּ֔ךָ

אֵ֥ל גָּד֖וֹל וְנוֹרָֽא׃

עליה ב׳

כב. וְנָשַׁל֩ יְהֹוָ֨ה אֱלֹהֶ֜יךָ

אֶת־הַגּוֹיִ֥ם הָאֵ֛ל

מִפָּנֶ֖יךָ מְעַ֣ט מְעָ֑ט

לֹ֤א תוּכַל֙ כַּלֹּתָ֣ם מַהֵ֔ר

פֶּן־תִּרְבֶּ֥ה עָלֶ֖יךָ חַיַּ֥ת הַשָּׂדֶֽה׃

כג. וּנְתָנָ֞ם

יְהֹוָ֤ה אֱלֹהֶ֙יךָ֙ לְפָנֶ֔יךָ

וְהָמָם֙ מְהוּמָ֣ה גְדֹלָ֔ה

עַ֖ד הִשָּׁמְדָֽם׃

כד. וְנָתַ֤ן מַלְכֵיהֶם֙ בְּיָדֶ֔ךָ

וְהַֽאֲבַדְתָּ֣ אֶת־שְׁמָ֔ם

מִתַּ֖חַת הַשָּׁמָ֑יִם

לֹֽא־יִתְיַצֵּ֥ב אִישׁ֙ בְּפָנֶ֔יךָ

עַ֥ד הִשְׁמִֽדְךָ֖ אֹתָֽם׃

31

לבדו יחיה האדם כי על כל מוצא
פי יהוה יחיה האדם שמלתך לא
בלתה מעליך ורגלך לא בצקה זה
ארבעים שנה וידעת עם לבבך כי
כאשר ייסר איש את בנו יהוה
אלהיך מיסרך ושמרת את מצות
יהוה אלהיך ללכת בדרכיו וליראה
אתו כי יהוה אלהיך מביאך אל ארץ
טובה ארץ נחלי מים עינת ותהמת
יצאים בבקעה ובהר ארץ חטה
ושערה וגפן ותאנה ורמון ארץ זית
שמן ודבש ארץ אשר לא במסכנת
תאכל בה לחם לא תחסר כל בה
ארץ אשר אבניה ברזל ומהרריה
תחצב נחשת ואכלת ושבעת וברכת
את יהוה אלהיך על הארץ הטבה
אשר נתן לך השמר לך פן תשכח
את יהוה אלהיך לבלתי שמר
מצותיו ומשפטיו וחקתיו אשר אנכי
מצוך היום פן תאכל ושבעת ובתים
טבים תבנה וישבת ובקרך וצאנך
ירבין וכסף וזהב ירבה לך וכל אשר
לך ירבה ורם לבבך ושכחת את
יהוה אלהיך המוציאך מארץ מצרים
מבית עבדים המוליכך במדבר הגדל

9. אֶרֶץ
אֲשֶׁר לֹא בְמִסְכֵּנֻת
תֹּאכַל־בָּהּ לֶחֶם
לֹא־תֶחְסַר כֹּל בָּהּ
אֶרֶץ אֲשֶׁר אֲבָנֶיהָ בַרְזֶל
וּמֵהֲרָרֶיהָ תַּחְצֹב נְחֹשֶׁת:

10. וְאָכַלְתָּ וְשָׂבָעְתָּ
וּבֵרַכְתָּ אֶת־יְהוָה אֱלֹהֶיךָ
עַל־הָאָרֶץ הַטֹּבָה
אֲשֶׁר נָתַן־לָךְ:

.4 שִׂמְלָתְךָ

לֹא בָלְתָה מֵעָלֶיךָ

וְרַגְלְךָ לֹא בָצֵקָה

זֶה אַרְבָּעִים שָׁנָה:

.5 וְיָדַעְתָּ עִם־לְבָבֶךָ

כִּי

כַּאֲשֶׁר יְיַסֵּר אִישׁ אֶת־בְּנוֹ

יהוה אֱלֹהֶיךָ מְיַסְּרֶךָּ:

.6 וְשָׁמַרְתָּ

אֶת־מִצְוֹת יהוה אֱלֹהֶיךָ

לָלֶכֶת בִּדְרָכָיו וּלְיִרְאָה אֹתוֹ:

.7 כִּי יהוה אֱלֹהֶיךָ

מְבִיאֲךָ אֶל־אֶרֶץ טוֹבָה

אֶרֶץ נַחֲלֵי מָיִם

עֲיָנֹת וּתְהֹמֹת

יֹצְאִים בַּבִּקְעָה וּבָהָר:

.8 אֶרֶץ חִטָּה וּשְׂעֹרָה

וְגֶפֶן וּתְאֵנָה וְרִמּוֹן

אֶרֶץ־זֵית שֶׁמֶן וּדְבָשׁ:

After the Torah reading, recite the following blessing.

בָּרוּךְ אַתָּה יְיָ אֱלֹהֵינוּ מֶלֶךְ הָעוֹלָם, אֲשֶׁר נָתַן לָנוּ תּוֹרַת אֱמֶת,

וְחַיֵּי עוֹלָם נָטַע בְּתוֹכֵנוּ. בָּרוּךְ אַתָּה יְיָ, נוֹתֵן הַתּוֹרָה.

We praise You, Adonai our God, Ruler of the universe,
Who planted eternal life among us by giving us a Teaching of truth.

We praise You, Adonai, the Giver of Torah.

TA'AMEI HA-MIKRA: TROP CHARTS

Let's face it: learning trop can be very difficult. Most of us are used to the idea that each musical sign represents a single tone, but with trop, most signs (ta'amim) represent musical phrases. To add to the difficulty, there are 28 separate trop signs — each with a unique musical phrase, and sometimes the phrasing changes depending on the combination of ta'amim (though very few readings contain all 28 ta'amim). Sure, you can find sheet music to help you out, but if you're like me and don't read music, you might wind up more confused. Oy!

I developed the charts in this section to help people like me. Most of the ta'amim are grouped into sequences that are used commonly in the Tanaḥ. The grids enable the teacher and the student to chart the music as it goes higher or lower.

These charts have proven quite helpful with my own students. I hope you find them just as useful!

אֶתְנַחְתָּא

Etnaḥta divides a verse into two broad ideas. Tipḥa, Zakef, Segol, and Shalshelet then divide Etnaḥta into smaller ideas. Etnaḥta always comes after Tipḥah.

Common Patterns
מֵירְכָא טִפְחָא מוּנַח אֶתְנַחְתָּא
טִפְחָא מוּנַח אֶתְנַחְתָּא
מֵירְכָא טִפְחָא אֶתְנַחְתָּא
טִפְחָא אֶתְנַחְתָּא
מוּנַח מוּנַח אֶתְנַחְתָּא

What's the point of all this trop?

Apart from musical notations, the trop (or, more properly, te'amim) tell us where to put the correct emphasis in each word and sentence. They also function as grammatical and syntactical notations, telling us when to pause in our reading, when to read quickly, etc. So we don't just read the punctuation — we sing it! There are seven distinct vocal systems for chanting the Tanaḥ. Most people are familiar with Torah and Haftarah. See if you can find out what the other five are!

TORAH TROP

Top section

(Grid with trope names written in the cells)

Common Patterns

סֶגּוֹל סוֹף־פָּסֽוּק
זָקֵף טִפְּחָ֖א סוֹף־פָּסֽוּק
זָקֵ֔ף אֶתְנַחְתָּ֑א
טִפְּחָ֖א אֶתְנַחְתָּ֑א סוֹף־פָּסֽוּק
טִפְּחָ֖א זָקֵף אֶתְנַחְתָּ֑א סוֹף־פָּסֽוּק
טִפְּחָ֖א סוֹף־פָּסֽוּק

סוֹף־פָּסֽוּק

Sof Pasuk is also called סִלּֽוּק (Siluk). It marks the end of a verse. Tipha and Zakef subdivide Sof Pasuk into smaller ideas. Sof Pasuk always comes after Tiphah.

Bottom section

(Grid with trope names written in the cells)

Common Patterns

אֶתְנַחְתָּ֑א טִפְּחָ֖א אֶתְנַחְתָּ֑א סֶגּוֹל
אֶתְנַחְתָּ֑א טִפְּחָ֖א אֶתְנַחְתָּ֑א
אֶתְנַחְתָּ֑א טִפְּחָ֖א זָקֵ֔ף
אֶתְנַחְתָּ֑א טִפְּחָ֖א אֶתְנַחְתָּ֑א
אֶתְנַחְתָּ֑א זָקֵף טִפְּחָ֖א אֶתְנַחְתָּ֑א
אֶתְנַחְתָּ֑א

אֶתְנַחְתָּ֑א

Etnahta divides a verse into two broad ideas. Tipha, Zakef, Segol, and Shalshelet then divide Etnahta into smaller ideas. Etnahta always comes after Tiphah.

TORAH TROP

Common Patterns

זָקֵף-קָטוֹן

Zakef divides Etnahta and Sof Pasuk into smaller ideas, but only if they already have a Tipha. Revi'a, Pashta and Yetiv suubdivide Zakef into even simpler ideas. Zakef-Katon (a.k.a Katon) is more common than Zakef-Gadol.

Common Patterns

תְּבִיר

When a Tipha idea has three or more words, it needs to be subdivided. We use Tevir for this subdivision.

TORAH TROP

Common Patterns

זָקֵף-גָּדוֹל

זָקֵף-גָּדוֹל

Zakef divides Etnahta and Sof Pasuk into smaller ideas, but only if they already have a Tipha. Revi'a, Pashta and Yetiv suubdivide Zakef into even simpler ideas. Zakef-Gadol is only found on short words and it never uses a Link.

Common Patterns

מְשָׁרֵת סֶגּוֹל אַזְלָא

מְשָׁרֵת זַרְקָא מְשָׁרֵת סֶגּוֹל

מְשָׁרֵת סֶגּוֹל

סֶגּוֹל

Segol divides Etnahta into smaller ideas, but only if it already has a Tipha and at least one Zakef, Revi'a, Pashta, Yetiv, and Zarka subdivide Segol into simpler ideas. Segol never appears on the first word of a verse.

TORAH TROP

Common Patterns

רְבִיעַֽ׃

מַחַת רְבִיעַ

מֵרְכָא רְבִיעַ | מַחְפַּ...

רְבִיעַ וּבַֽתַ...

רְבִיעַ

When Tipha, Zakef, or Segol need to be subdivided and they have one or two Tevirs, Revï'a is used as the Divider.

Common Patterns

גֵּרֵֽשׁ

קַדְמָ אַזְלָֽ׳ גֵּרֵֽשׁ

זֵ׳ קַדְמָ אַזְלָֽ (a.k.a. אַזְלָֽ גֵּרֵֽשׁ)

גֵּרֵֽשׁ זֵ׳ קַדְמָ אַזְלָֽ

קַדְמָ אַזְלָֽ זֵ׳ קַדְמָ וּפַשְׁטָ-אַשְׁלֵֽי...

גֵּרֵֽשׁ

If a Tevir, Pashta, Revï'a or Zarka needs to be subdivided, the subdivider is usually Geresh or Gershayim.

TORAH TROP

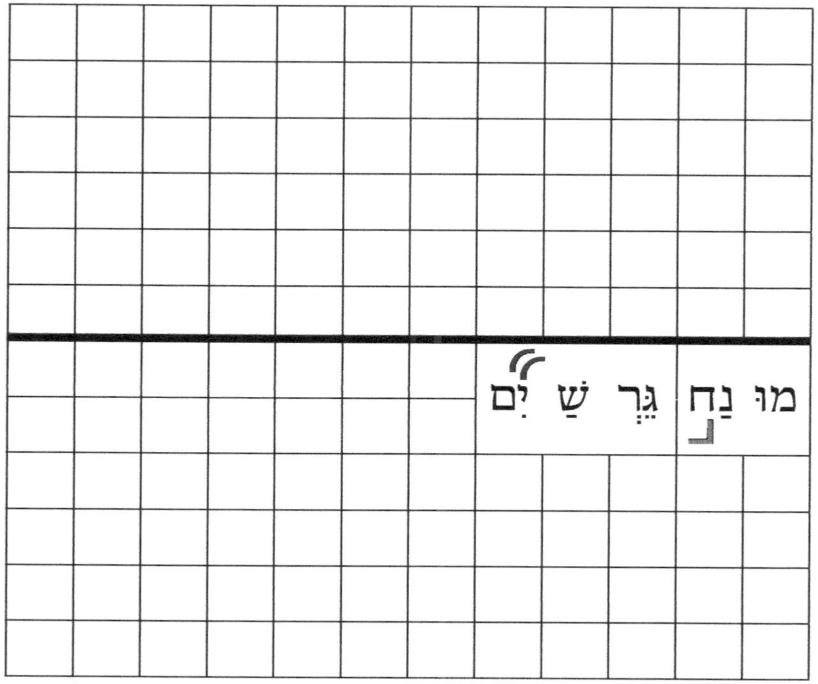

(Right section — Pashta / Yetiv)

פַּשְׁטָא ◌ׄ

וְיָ֫י גִּ֫ל עָ֫י

וְיַֽי ◌ׄ

וְיָ֫י מֵ֫י בֵּ֫ר

גִּ֫ל עָ֫י ◌ׄ

Common Patterns

יְתִ֚ב

יְתִ֚ב טֹ֖וב

יְתִ֚ב מֵ֣תָה טֹ֖וב

בְּשֶׁ֚עַ אֹ֖ו (rare)

(Left section — Gershayim)

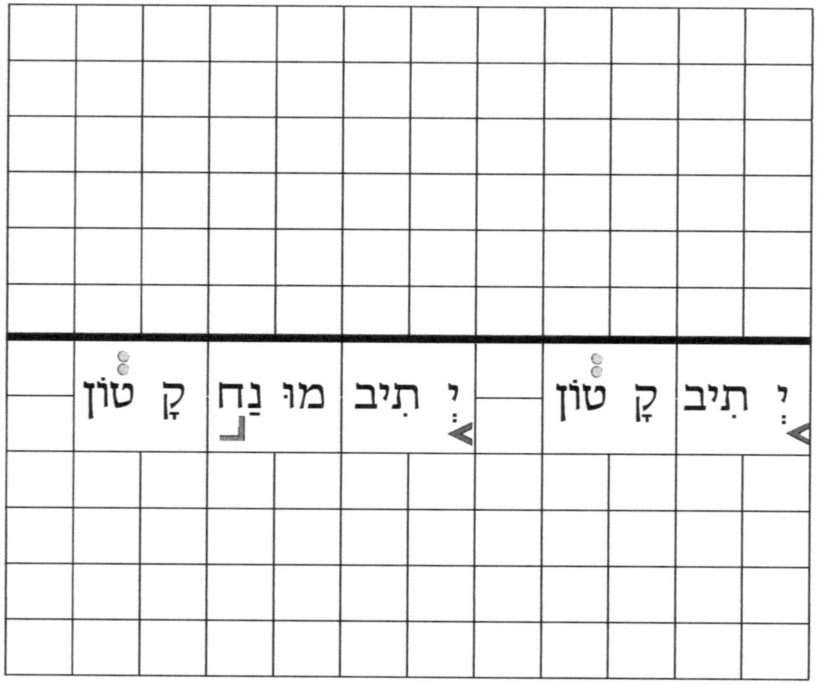

בֵּ֜ר לֵ֜י בָ֜ו מֹ֜ו עַ֜י

Common Patterns

גֵּרְשַׁ֜יִם

גֵּרְשַׁ֜יִם מֵ֣תָה

TORAH TROP

Common Patterns
מוּנַּח פָּזֵר

פָּזֵר

Pazer is used to subdivide Tevir, Revi'a, Pashta, and Zarka. Pazer can be linked to up to six Munahs.

Common Patterns
מוּנַּח תְּלִישָׁא־גְדוֹלָה

תְּלִישָׁא־גְדוֹלָה

When Tevir, Revi'a, Pashta, or Zarka need to be subdivided. Telishah-Gedolah is sometimes used. When the accent is not on the first syllable, a second Telishah-Gedolah is often added to mark the stress. Telishah-Gedolah can be linked to up to six Munahs.

40

D'VAR TORAH WRITING GUIDE

This guide is intended to give you a general idea of what a typical D'var Torah looks like. Yours may not look exactly like this — it will, of course, be written by you and not me! — but it should include all of these elements. As always, make sure you consult with your rabbi / teacher.

1. Don't thank people for coming — that's something you can tell your guests at the party afterwards. The person giving the D'var Torah is called a *Darshan* — literally, an "explainer". The congregation will thank *you* for explaining the weekly readings to *them*.

2. In one or two paragraphs, summarize the content of the Torah and Haftarah readings for that day.

3. Quote a verse or idea from the Torah and/or Haftarah in Hebrew and in English, and discuss its relevance in our times. This is when you bring in your own commentaries and tell us what you've learned from our ancient and modern teachers.

4. Explain how the idea you've chosen has meaning to you. You can discuss the impact the D'var Torah may have had on how you're going to lead your life, how it's affected your commitment to Judaism and its values, etc.

5. If it fits with your ideas, you may want to talk about your parents, grandparents or other family members and role models and what positive values or lessons you've learned from them. Note: this is not the same as thanking them. Save the "thank you's" for after the service!

6. Final thoughts: what does becoming a Bar/Bat Mitzvah mean to you? Why is it special to you and what have you learned in the process of studying for today? Typically, this is where you bring your discussion back to the original idea you chose from the Torah / Haftarah.

7. Your D'var Torah should be no more than four or five double-spaced pages — roughly the length of a five to seven minute speech.

My **parashah**, book from the Torah, and chapter/verse

My **Haftarah** book and chapter/verse reference...

What the TORAH says in my own words:

What the HAFTARAH says in my own words:

Questions I have about my TORAH reading, Haftarah, Bar/Bat Mitzvah process, or Judaism in general (minimum 3):	Questions my parents have about my TORAH reading, Haftarah, Bar/Bat Mitzvah process, or Judaism in general (minimum 3):

SECTIONS OF TORAH THAT STAND OUT FOR ME...

Chapter : Verse OR Section	What it says in my own words	Why it stands out for me

SECTIONS OF HAFTARAH THAT STAND OUT FOR ME...

Chapter : Verse OR Section	What it says in my own words	Why it stands out for me
↑	↑	
↑	↑	
↑	↑	

One idea or theme I want to talk about (based on my choices from charts 3 and 4):	
Verse or section from the Torah or Haftarah that relates to my theme (choose 1 or 2 from charts 3 and/or 4 and write them here):	

Commentator	The commentator's own words	What I think the commentator is trying to teach

One idea or theme I want to talk about: (copy from previous chart)	
Verse or section from the Torah or Haftarah that relates to my theme: (copy from previous chart)	

Commentator (copy from previous chart)	What I think the commentator is trying to teach (copy from previous chart)	How this teaching relates to my life or the world around me
↑	↑	
↑	↑	
↑	↑	

One idea or theme I want to talk about:
(copy from previous chart)

Verse or section from the Torah or Haftarah that relates to my theme:
(copy from previous chart)

Commentator
(copy from previous chart)

How this teaching relates to my life or the world around me
(copy from previous chart)

My lesson for this parashah (bring all your ideas together)

INCREDIBLY HANDY TIME LINE

The dates here are approximate. The two main columns compare the Tanah's chronology with samples of writings from ancient Yisra'el's neighbors that relate to events in the Tanah. There are also thousands of Hebrew inscriptions and documents dug up by archeologists, but unfortunately I don't have space to mention them all! The narrow column on the left shows you when the books of the Torah and *Nevi'im* (Prophets) <u>take place</u>, **not** <u>when they were written</u>. See if you can locate your own Torah / Haftarah readings on this time line!

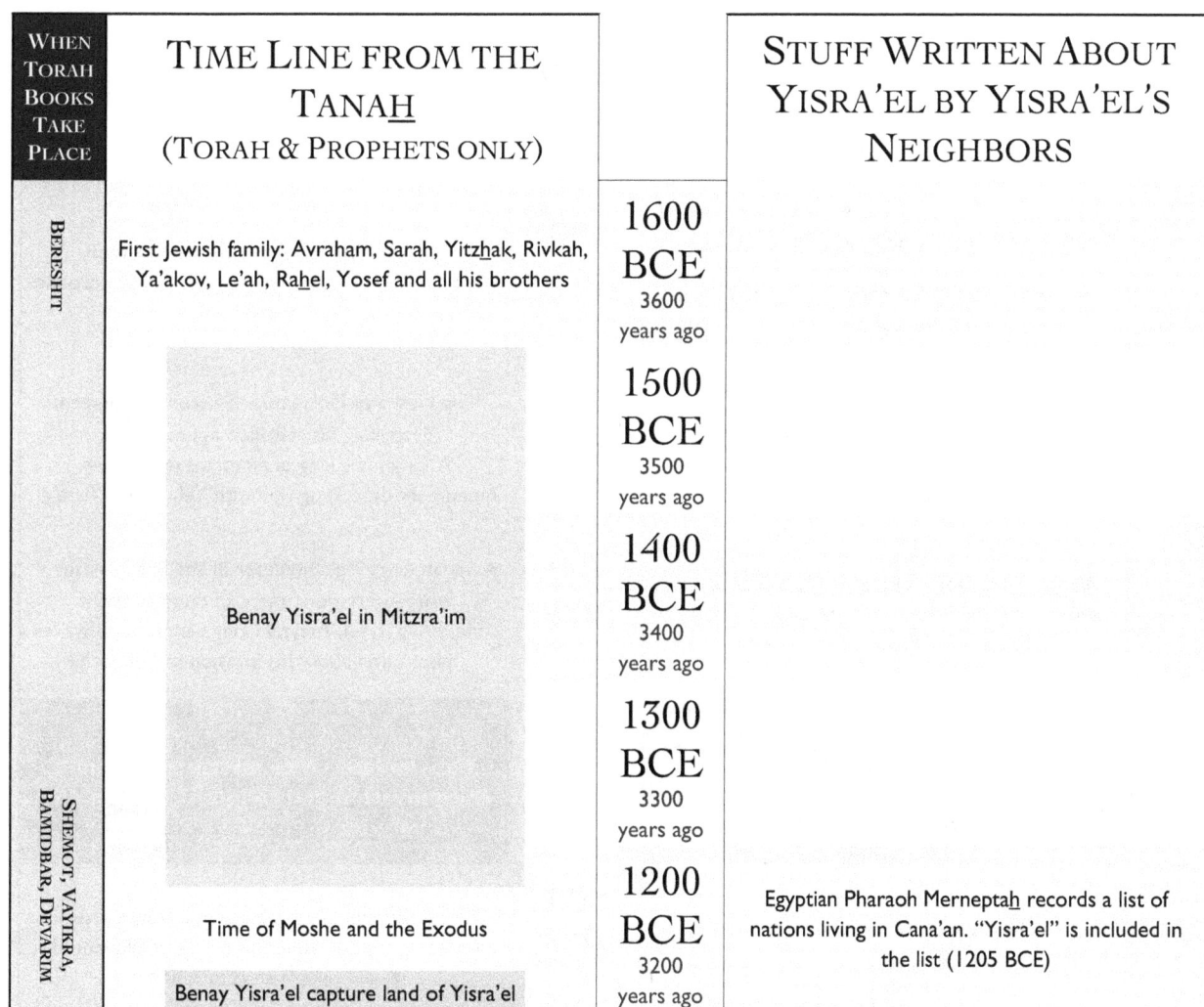

WHEN TORAH BOOKS TAKE PLACE	TIME LINE FROM THE TANAH (TORAH & PROPHETS ONLY)		STUFF WRITTEN ABOUT YISRA'EL BY YISRA'EL'S NEIGHBORS
BERESHIT	First Jewish family: Avraham, Sarah, Yitzhak, Rivkah, Ya'akov, Le'ah, Rahel, Yosef and all his brothers	**1600 BCE** 3600 years ago	
		1500 BCE 3500 years ago	
	Benay Yisra'el in Mitzra'im	**1400 BCE** 3400 years ago	
		1300 BCE 3300 years ago	
SHEMOT, VAYIKRA, BAMIDBAR, DEVARIM	Time of Moshe and the Exodus	**1200 BCE** 3200 years ago	Egyptian Pharaoh Merneptah records a list of nations living in Cana'an. "Yisra'el" is included in the list (1205 BCE)
	Benay Yisra'el capture land of Yisra'el		

When *Navi* Books Take Place		1200 BCE 3200 years ago	Egyptian Pharaoh Merneptah records a list of nations living in Cana'an. "Yisra'el" is included in the list (1205 BCE)
Yehoshu'a, Shoftim	Benay Yisra'el in Mitzra'im Time of Moshe and the Exodus Benay Yisra'el capture the land of Yisra'el and settle it. Time of the *Shoftim* (tribal chiefs).	1100 BCE 3100 years ago	
Shemu'el	Time of King Sha'ul, King David and King Shlomo; First Temple is built; Kingdom of Yisra'el established	1000 BCE 3000 years ago	
1 Melahim	Kingdom splits into Yehudah and Yisra'el (922 BCE) Book of *1 Melahim* describes invasion of Yehudah by Pharaoh Shishak	900 BCE 2900 years ago	Egyptian Pharaoh Shishak writes a victory monument about invading the region in and around Yisra'el
2 Melahim Amos, Hoshe'a, Nahum, Micah, Yish'ayah #1	Time of Eliyahu and Elisha; Book of *2 Melahim* describes a rebellion against Yisra'el by Mesha, king of Mo'ab; *2 Melahim* also describes war between Aram, Yehudah, and Yisra'el	800 BCE 2800 years ago	King Mesha of Mo'ab makes a stone monument describing his rebellion against Israel; Anonymous king of Aram makes a stone monument describing war with Yehudah & Yisra'el
	Ashur conquers Yisra'el (722-720 BCE) Books of *2 Melahim* and *Yish'ayah* describe Assyrian invasions of Yehudah and Yisra'el	700 BCE 2700 years ago	Assyrian kings Tiglath-Pileser III and Shalmaneser V write inscriptions and wall carvings about conquering Israel; Assyrian king Sennacherib writes inscription about his invasion of Yehudah
2 Melahim Tzefanyah, Yirmiyah, Yehezk'el, Yish'ayah #2, Ovadyah	**Bavel conquers Yehudah (590's-586 BCE)** Yerushalayim destroyed (586 BCE)	600 BCE 2600 years ago	**Babylonians write inscriptions about their invasion and conquest of Yehudah**
Hagai, Zeharyah, Habakuk, Mal'ahi	Cyrus of Persia allows exiles to return from Bavel; Temple rebuilt; time of Nehemiyah & Ezra	500 BCE 2500 years ago	Persia conquers Babylon; Persian King Cyrus II writes inscription about his policy of allowing all exiled people to return home

WHEN *NAVI* BOOKS TAKE PLACE				
HAGAI, ZEHARYAH, HABAKUK, MAL'AHI	Cyrus of Persia allows exiles to return from Bavel; Temple rebuilt; time of Nehemiyah & Ezra		**500 BCE** 2500 years ago	Persia conquers Babylon; Persian King Cyrus II writes inscription about his policy of allowing all exiled people to return home
			400 BCE 2400 years ago	
		Books of the Torah, Prophets, and other pieces of literature are edited and compiled into the Tanah	**300 BCE** 2300 years ago	Greek Empire defeats Persia and takes control of the land of Israel
		Jews successfully rebel against Greek Seleucid Empire & establish kingdom of Judea (Hanukah)	**200 BCE** 2200 years ago	
			100 BCE 2100 years ago	
	Time of the Mishnah (final compilation roughly 200 CE)			Dead Sea Scrolls are written and hidden in caves in the Judean Desert · Roman Empire takes control of Judea
		Jews rebel against Rome; Jerusalem and the Temple are destroyed (70 CE)	**1 BCE / 1 CE** 2000 years ago	**Romans build a massive arch with carvings that depict the victory over the Jews**
			200 CE 1800 years ago	

www.ingramcontent.com/pod-product-compliance
Lightning Source LLC
Chambersburg PA
CBHW081231020426
42331CB00012B/3119